Sunflower

By Kimberly Rochelle

Sunflower

By Kimberly Rochelle

Dedication

This book is dedicated

to my King.

May we speak

in the language of flowers

forever and always.

Sunflower

The sunflower for quite
some time now has been
the most beautiful sight to
see.

You see she is strong,
stands boldly with
strength and poise.

So tall you basked in the
shade she gently provides
as she rises to touch the
sky just so the Sun itself
could admire her beauty.

When you're in her
presence you won't be
able to help but notice
how refreshed and at
peace you are.

Finally pure happiness.

Testimonials

Sunflower

About being the light energy and support for others the way Sunflowers shine with each other amidst the storms of life:

Such a positive outlook on life that inspires me every day!

- Curtis E.

Ma'am, you are very kindhearted. I want to become just like you, you are my biggest inspiration! When I was lost no one was there for me, then I came to know about your live sessions on the 8th of July.

Your guidance helped me a lot, you came as an Angel in my life and your guidance brought me out of my darkness. Sometimes I think of giving up but then I remember your positive words said in the live [session] and I become motivated. Thanks a lot, dear, ma'am.

- Sakshi S.

She is very positive in life and what it has to offer her and is a very nice young woman.

- Annemarie D.

Kimberly is the sweetest soul. She helped me through a life-changing decision in my marriage while also focusing on healing myself from the inside. Each session with her left me feeling at peace and focused.

- Amanda E.

Since I have known Kimberly, she has always been my go-to person. She is well known for her personality. So, friendly and kind to everyone. She always knows what to say to get through and is so positive. I could not have made it through without her friendship, kindness, positive bubbly personality, and her overall caring soul. I highly recommend her!

- Savannah H.

I try to see you every day you come on live. You told me 2 days ago about you could see the mint wall being painted and an elephant, my daughter told me today her boyfriend painted the bedroom for the baby mint wall jungle theme guess what there's an elephant!
Spot-on Kim xx

- Belinda M.

Sunflower

Kimberly went above and beyond to help us, WE WILL follow her. Positive attitude and like I said, she went above and beyond to help us and I made a new friend.

- Virginia C.

I credit Kim, along with one other individual, with preventing my suicide. I was in a horribly dark place, spending over $1500 a week on opiates and whatever else would make the pain go away.

Kimberly was working at a hotel on the grave shift at this time, but no matter what, she always replied to my messages and would always offer me a cup of coffee.

She never judged me and would let me ramble for hours.

- Daniel B.

That's amazing advice. Love & light. Thank you.

- Anonymous

She is a nice/kind, very helpful, knowledgeable, non-pressuring yet effective, positive attitude on work and life in general, and an all-around caring person. Kim makes people around her feel comfortable no matter the circumstance.

- Mark G.

She was very organized and very caring and very explanatory meaning she was able to explain every detail of a reading that she did for me, and everything was accurate.

- Vanessa R.

She is that girl to get it done from. She is great with timing too. I had a meeting we had the meeting for 11:30 she was on time. Just everything was just wonderful with her. So, like I said, I recommend her, she's perfect.

- Merra S.

Thank you. Resonates so much lovely.

- Anonymous

Sunflower

The Growth of a Sunflower

Preface

Once upon a time…

There once was
a boy named Tejaswi
he always tried his best
to be good to all.

Time after time again
other people just let
him fall.

He prayed for a sign
that he was on the
right path.

Then he stumbled
upon a girl,
just like that.

She was funny
and bright, she
let up his life

but he dare not
talk to her,
what would he say?

If too direct would
She ghost him
denying his friendship
she just may.

So he waited and waited
patiently so
dropping hints giving flowers
hoping one day she'd know.

A few months went by
she felt all alone
then looked up and saw
a single flower being shown.

He makes me smile
even when I'm feeling blue
then one day she said unexpectedly
'I love you.'

No she didn't know him
or how to say his name
she saw his kindness
and could love him
through her own pain.

Then something happened
and things were never the same.

Sunflower

He showed her self-worth,
she did the same.
They began a love story
neither would want to tame.

They danced, laughed and played
until one day they claimed,
I am yours, you are mine
now we share a last name

This was just the beginning
of this fairytale love.

When two people are worthy
they'll find a something special
sent from above.

Sunflower and Marigold: A Love Story

Introduction

This journey stemmed from a story of love.

Sunflowers have always resonated with me because they stand tall and proud even if they're the only one of their kind around.

The sunflower was my guide on my spiritual journey for many years as they always point to the light.

With a sunflower planted in front of me I knew I would always head in the right direction.

It wasn't until recently I learned one of my favorite facts about these amazing beings:

When there is no sunshine in the sky, the Sunflowers look toward each other as if to receive the positive energy they need from another just like them.

A few weeks after I learned that my life sprung the most beautiful soul inspiring relationship on me, my King.

He is who referred to me Sunflower for months before I noticed his existence.

Not every time we faced together was filled
with light and love.

In fact, I was facing a lot of shadows when
we met, but nonetheless when times were
dark, he was the sunflower I needed to keep
my energy high when no sun was in the sky.

He believed in me, supported me and
encouraged me to write this book.

The poems stem from the innocence we
share but take a journey through my healing
process.

All the light, dark and in-between.

Sunflower

The Seedling

I'm not sure why I am here.

What is the purpose of my existence?

I wish I knew.

There is so much to this world, I feel it
although I've never experienced it firsthand.

All I've done is stayed here in this spot.

I like my ways, this shell keeps me safe.

Underground, here I am out of harms way.

I can't help but wonder, though,
am I destined for more?

What would happen if instead of shutting
down, I bravely walk
through the open door?

Who am I kidding?

I am not a brave soul.

I'll just sit here and develop and watch
myself grow.

I am alone in this world, haven't met
another soul like mine.

Sunflower

Perhaps I will one day, when I am brave enough to cross that line.

However, that day isn't today, and I'm okay with that.

Perhaps that day I'll embark on that adventure I once thought I could have.

Oh, wouldn't that be so wonderful?

Living my life fearlessly.

But right now I can't, the fear is all I see.

I'll stay in my shell, for a month.

Maybe two.

Put down roots then see what my life comes to once I have courage to be myself and the audacity to express the authentic me.

Is that even possible to do as a seedling?

I guess we'll see.

Safety

Do you feel
protected?

No.

Well,
you are.

I started noticing
invisible barriers
surrounding my space.

I am

Protected.

Sunflower

Fight or Flight

I'm so scared,
I have a tendency
of running away.

I'm also very tired
of running.

The entire time,
though,

I've been running
to you.

Human

What is this?
Flesh and bone.

Is there more?
I feel, I think,

I see all.
There is more.

We are all.
All the joy,

all the energy,
we are everything!

Create the world
you want to live.

The change is here!
One by one.

Hand in hand.
By simple humans.

Sunflower

Guided Conversation

I glanced
at myself in the mirror.

My eyes
twinkled.

She is about
to change the world,
one said.

Love,
she changes the world
every day.

Another replied,
just by being her.

Heart Noises

I listened
to my heart opening

as the birds chirped
early that morning.

That day
I found myself.

Unseen rainbows
covering the clouded
moonlit sky.

You're here,
I'm here.

I am.

Sunflower

Rooting in

Settling into my ways
wherever I am,
here or there.

I'll be strong.

…I think.

I'll stand my ground.

…I hope.

I'll speak with confidence.
Or at least,
I'll try.

I'm a being too
I deserve to shine.

Alas I stay here
in the dark
the cold
my fears

Sunflower

the same place I've been
for almost 30 years.

Getting used to the cold.
I'm used to the dark.
I'm twisted in ways
only known as art.

No matter what happens,
where I go,
or who I see,

I'll stay true to my heart.
Maybe one day
I'll feel like me

Integration

I felt the energy
come inside.

Who are you?
He asked.

I smiled and said,
"Welcome to the game."

Sunflower

Midnight Meditation

I meditated before bed
it was magical.

I created a whole new world
in which I can escape to.

A world of my very own
that is mine to create.

During this session
I started out
doing some running
through the forest.

No shoes on,
none needed
the ground was soft
under my quick feet.

I'm very agile,
I love weaving
through the trees.

Then I came to a clearing
I laid and looked at the clouds.

Fresh lavender
surrounded me
the scent filled my nose.

I floated up
and played with

gusts of wind
for a bit before
coming back.

I had a fantastic time,
I can't wait to go back.
Maybe in my sleep.

Sunflower

New Moon Child

I am cloaked
in darkness.

I raised my hands
like a phantom

making the most
eerie noise

I could muster.

You're still not scary

He said,
unphased.

Sound Therapy

I felt myself
being pulled back
into my body

like my soul
was being grabbed
by octopus tentacles

until I returned
to my rightful place.

Me.

Sunflower

Hopping Birds Fly

"You're grounded now,"
the bird said

as she hopped around
on the grass.

"I am grounding,
I'm getting there."

"No," she said,
"you're grounded now."

Hop hop hop.

"Just remember
you still have wings

and you can fly
whenever you want,"

she reminded me.

Another bird hopped toward her,
they both flew off together.

The Only Constant

Change
your ways.

Your thoughts,
your patterns,

your ways
of life;

everything.

Sunflower

Are you ready?

I've been so good
I just now can see

I try so hard
but am familiar to chaos.

If everything went right,
when everything goes right,

will I know to bend?
Can I take the pressure?

I've been made for this
always was my destiny.

Precipitation & Condensation

Air oddly cool
sky all shades of blue.

Hairs a mess,
outfit frumpy too.

Fluffy white clouds-

Sometimes rain pours
purification of the soul.

But at times of healing

things must arise.
They blow on the wind

dancing, changing.

Showering us so
we can show the world

it's okay to let go.

Sunflower

Breaking the Shell

Alas, I have grown.

I didn't want to, nor did I try but nonetheless
it has happened. My shell is starting to split.

I want to cry.

I have no idea what is next for me.

My dark comfort zone is now allowing the
damp surroundings to penetrate my flesh.

Am I broken?

Can't I do anything right?!

Why must everything I touch break?

…including myself.

The darkness is closer. I feel colder.

More distant from my core.

Everything is oh so overwhelming.

Am I living in love or fear?

The lines so blurred I cannot tell anymore.

Sunflower

There is More.

I'm hanging in limbo
2 weeks gone by
being stretched back.

Now launching forward
feels so slow
these precise movements

I feel accurate
moments before
arrow to be released

Take a breath in
and breathe it out.
All is still.

Time to let go.

Let the Darkness Rise

Release the beasts
the wolves all howl.
Half nights moon
terrifying scowl.

I look at you,
you smirk at me,
it's on instinctively.
No 1, 2, or 3.

Let the dark night
rain it's terror above.
The stars are hiding
no light for us.

Clouds dance mischievously,
where have they gone?
The bats squeak and squawk
most terrifying songs

Sunflower

Bite marks, blood shed
it's all in good fun
Hail the darkness
'til we see the Sun.

We run the night
all others run in fear.
Spooks and goblins are out
just friends my dear.

The darkness is good
although looks really glim.
Be one with all
including your menacing grin.

Good, love and light.
Evil, hate and dark.
Embrace it all
One journey embarked.

You are no angel,
no demon either.
A God is both,
human is neither.

Clarifying Winds

Everything
is flowing together now

It all makes sense

Like the wind we blow
Living one moment
to the next

I completely
understand

Where I belong

Right here, in this moment
Nothing can go wrong.

Sunflower

The Mirror

The north star
always pointing me
in the right way.

I reached out
grabbed the glass
it's just a mirror.

The entire time
the light was
within me.

Hares on Edge

Rabbits and bunnies
dashing side to side.
Some floppy eared
some standing high.

Brown ones, white ones
black haired ones too-
Listen to their paths
yours just may find you.

Their silence speaks loudly

nuzzling their way
eating lots of fruits
veggies and greens
along the way

A hopping good time
fun, reproduction
homes filled with May

Sunflower

So much to do,
so much to see.

But for now,
take their words silently.

Allowing their messages
to flow freely.

Known for agility
and listening calmly

Now understand why
these creatures
are considered to be

so lucky.

How Dare She.

I'm just a girl

who isn't scared
to be herself.

The audacity.

Sunflower

The Mound

A pile of rocks and dirt
growing green with life.

I'm not sure
can I do this? Doubt.

He looked at me, smiled.
Hand reaching toward mine.

Will you come over this?
Overcome, I corrected.

The camera panned out
showing the mound
as just a mound.

Now, will you come over?
I grabbed his hand,

took one step and
found myself at the top.

The sun kissed my face
it warmed my soul.

Can't let this get us.
Please trust me,

I have a plan.
& I knew he did.

Sunflower

Perfect Miracles

They happen every day
if you witnessed a miracle
what would you say?

Would you stand speechless?
Could you talk at all?

If you saw a world around you
trees standing tall

Would you notice the wonder,
the natural Miracles in it all?

The children laughing
leaves changing in the fall.

Each blade of grass
giving shelter and shade.
Or notice at shopping malls
how every life is made.

With wondrous skills
the sparkles in their eyes.
That's how miracle are made
in all shapes and size.

Sprouting

Sunflower

To feel the slightest warmth from the Sun on my skin after being buried so long in the cold, dark, damp ground I've become so accustomed to.

Did I ever belong here?

I started putting down roots, but was I ever meant to stay?

I wonder now that I am getting warmer, the bright beginnings that I feel are coming my way.

Were we ever meant to stay in our confides of comfort zones? Or is there an entirely new world I have no idea about just a few pushes away.

I feel the answers to all I've bee looking for are within my grasp.

I'm extremely terrified but something is telling me to keep pushing.

Go forward.

Fight through the darkness and breach the surface of the world I was meant to *always* be a part of.

The kind, gentle warmth of the sun.

The swaying with the winds.

The rain washing away impurities from my petals.

Is this place real?

This entire time, I thought it to be a fairytale.

But what if it wasn't?

What if it's not?!

Can I push a little further and have everything I've ever thought I couldn't?

Let's see.

Sunflower

Scared to See.

I heard a ruckus from behind.
Two brown birds trying to balance

on my rear wiper
one had a leaf in his mouth.

"We're building a nest," said the other.
"Want to see it?" She asked.

"Not yet," I replied.
Farewells and gone away.

Facing Fears

I held my fears
in the palms of my hands.

I put them to my heart
and held them close.

I blessed them
and kissed my hands.

As I held my breath
and shut my eyes.

I made a wish,
one great in size.

I held my hands out
opened them and blew.

Opening my eyes now
seeing something new.

Sunflower

Wish turning into green,
glittery powder.
Glistens being swept away
by a passing gust of wind.

I let the wind surround me,
I spread my arms preparing to fly.

I took a deep
cleansing breath in,
and let go.

I was at peace.
I am not scared anymore.

I jumped.

Conversations with Birds

I walked outside
and the birds chirped

"She has risen."

Sunflower

Natural Earth

The door opens
blue jay soaring across path.
Yes, throat has been freed!

The air still crisp
damp morning dew.

Mystical sunrises
birds chirping too.

Greenery everywhere

Heart, new moon.
white flowered bushes
innocently bloom.

We sniff the air,
there's nothing there.
Yellow stillness, tickly nose.

All birds chirping
robins, finches, and crows.

Pale blue sky
not a cloud in sight

Misty mornings taught
Earth lessons from above

Machines rumble
birds of wire.
We're all one, I am all.

Piles of rocks
cold, solid, dense
splash against.

Waters of the trench
sedimentation,
he breaks in two

We're all of Earth
no more no less
once you take flight

we can save her
from this mess.

I'm as you are
stand up and see.

The magical world
right in front of thee.

Sunflower

Constant Growth

I feel my heart beating hard.

It's been a fairytale
from the beginning,
but the growth must go on.

The Dance of Growth

With every step
I ground.

With every movement
I dance.

With every breath
I align.

With every word
I trust.

With every moment
I embrace

With every taste
I indulge

With every action
I manifest

I am forever centered
on my divine path.

Sunflower

Rays and shine.

Every time I see the Sun
may it's rays fill me in
with light, love, joy
happiness, and peace.

May I know the Sun's warmth
even on the cloudiest, coldest
rainstorm-iest days.

& Forever know
the light I bring
to the world and the lives
of those around me.

Innocence

Sunflower

I've never seen this stuff before…

The dew,

the rain,

the sky,

the birds.

Isn't the world wonderful?

A beautiful Spring Summer Day

Making friends with the bugs

who crawl around saying hello.

Life is amazing,

every day a wonder.

I don't see how

it could be any fun-er.

The Rising Sun

As the sun rose
marking the start
of the new era

the darkness fled
from every blade of grass
never to rule the day.

This is a new beginning
the flowers may now grow
bringing beauty
to the natural world.

Sunflower

Dandelion Fields

A field of beautiful blooms.

What most cut away
deem as pests and weeds,

I see a land of possibilities.

Children's Tales

Finger paint and bubbles
cookies and messes
these are the ingredients
to create happy children.

Outside sunshine
sprinklers and water
skipping rocks
tall trees, exploring

from parent to kids
we're all trying our best.
Bath time, movies, cuddles
lots of kisses, upsets

tummy tickles,
laughter giggles
worlds of play,
do not deny

everything is real.

Sunflower

Teach them, ethics
morals, strengths
praise their talents
and creative sides

you know what to do
show them you care
and no matter what happens
you'll always be there.

Adorable Exploration

Knock knock
little one
opens the door.

"Come play,"
says he eagerly.

He grabs her hand
Where to go?
A whole new world

only our
imaginations know

magnifying glass
bees, fairies, frogs
trippy roots

I your princess
you're my prince.

Sunflower

Messy pigtails
mud on jeans
creating a world

more magical
than it seems.

Look closer,
see all the bugs?

Trees give shelter,
butterflies give hugs.

The softest moss
everything's green.

Two 4-year-olds
know everything.

Rebirth

As spring emerges
and life re-emerges
as brand new

you breathe new life into my soul.
I love how crisp the air is up here

like no other
I can finally breathe.

I am me.

Sunflower

Grandmother's Stars

"You are so beautiful,"
I told the Moon.

"You're even more so,"
She responded.

"I thank my lucky stars
to have you shining for me,"
she continued.

"I bet you have
a whole lot
of lucky stars."

I smiled

"I have an entire galaxy
filled with them,"

She explained

"and a universe
filled with even more!"

"That's a lot of luck!
May each one
spread the joy
where it's needed."

"That's exactly why
I love you."

Sunflower

Self-acceptance

There comes a time
when you just want to
be set free.

Sometimes we don't have
the courage to do this
on our own.

That's where you came in
you encouraged every
little thing I do.

From goofing off
singing, dancing, writing
and much more!

You said each aspect
is absolutely perfect
you want more.

The more I preformed
the more comfortable
I became

with whom I am
I create myself
through expression.

The entire time
you accepted

every aspect

of who I am inside.
Soon, I realized

I did too.

Sunflower

Wind Spirit

I cannot be swayed
For I am the Wind.

Changes in the Winds

Sunflower

When did this fairytale

turn into a nightmare?

All I did was exist

then all of a sudden

the darkness I thought I left behind

turned into a thick mist

It rose so high

all around me

I forgot I could see.

There are dark shadows

moving in the distance.

What?

Who could they be?

I rise.

I fall.

I twist, dip, and turn.

When will this rollercoaster be over

my mind, my body yearns.

Changes in the air

for good or worse.

I thought everything was going well

Now seems like a curse.

Sunflower

First Flight

Eyes closed
chirps and tweets
gentle breezes
arms out wide

I feel it.
The wind
beneath
my wings.

I'm flying,
I sing.

Watch me soar
I'm a bird
Forever more.

Expanding Perception

I spun around as a kid screaming
"I'm a tornado!"
I then understood,
No, I'm a tree.
I only sway and bend in the wind
but never break.

I see now, I'm grounded.
I am a tree, right?
This out of control storm at sister's,
I turned into a treehouse.
May there be blessings, flowers,
Sunshine. Blessed be.

A cosmic explosion creating a
plain far and wide.
Add a tuff of green grass
just for some life.
Sun so high, warm and bright
clouds & wind for weather.

Let's see how she grows.

Sunflower

The Ever-changing Sky

I looked up to the sun
peeking through the clouds.

He said I'll be here
shining for you every day.

I smiled.

Chaotic Winds

The storm
raged around me.

Rain falling left.
Lightening made the sky
seem as if it were still day.

"I embrace the storm,"
I said.
Thunder clapped,

once,
twice,
three times.

I laughed.

Sunflower

Embracing the Time

I sat with my eyes closed
feeling earth's energy rise
up my leg channels
tickling as it cleansed.

The birds chirping
vehicles whirring
down nearby streets.

What do you hear?
I tried to block out
manmade noises,
"birds and life around me."

"Is that all?" "No."
I added back humanity
"I hear movement."

"Go on, continue."
"I hear traction
I hear the motors
giving life to machine."

"Good.
You are here.
You live in this age.
Embrace all you hear."

I then understood,
the world is much bigger
than what I let into mine.

"I embrace humanity.

I embrace this day in age.
The world never seemed so vast
am I really this small?"
"No, you are it all."

Sunflower

Persistence

Wherever you are
keep going,
don't stop there.

A Moment with Sun

I glanced up toward the Sun setting
behind tree branches.
He said, "I like the look."
"I thought I'd shine for you for a change."
"I like it."

I turned to see my reflection
in a nearby window.

A bright yellow dress
round glasses framed by gold.

I smiled.

Sunflower

Learning to Trust

Trust.
Like a jump
some compare
to falling.

How far does it go?
The depth, how deep?
The entire extent…

Those who believe
falling will happen
will always fall.

Babe,
since you
I've never soared
so high.

The idea of falling
Its laughable. Ha!
Never with you.

I can't get enough
I'll trust until
the end of time.

The Bud

Sunflower

I've been growing rapidly, stretching in unfamiliar ways.

Yet something seems so calm and familiar about the Sun's shining rays.

I feel so different than I did just a few months ago.

Those walls I was stuck in for so long ultimately helped me grow.

I didn't understand at the time, but my roots were helping me stay strong. For there is more than just Sun, wind and rain here; Earth has a beautiful song.

The vibrations I feel the chirping of the birds have made me grow in ways, I cannot express in words.

I see so much life!

Green grass, butterflies, bumblebees.

They go to so many other flowers, but why
do they always skip me?

Am I not worthy of their attention and love?

Do I come from another place?

I know I'm just a stem, much thicker than
the flowers surrounding me. But I promise
I'm colorful on the inside, I can feel the
beauty I consist of.

Finally, outside the surface of cold dark
Earth, I see this life, but I feel so alone.

Please dear Universe, send me someone I
can call my own.

They mustn't be perfect, because well,
neither am I.
Thought I was a flower but here I am a
simple stem aiming for the sky.

Sunflower

Tree People

I placed my left hand
on the cold, damp bark.

"I have a lot to give you,
are you ready to receive?"

"I am."

I felt the energy
flow into me…

"That's it?" I asked.
It didn't seem like much.

"It's all a matter
of perception, remember?"

"Yes," I nodded.

"Oh,

may I have
some trust too please?"

"You may already have it,"
he smiled.

I smiled back
and understood.

Doubt

"Can I trust?"
He lovingly assured
"When will you realize?

You see this?"
He adjusted the crown.

Indeed
he is my King.

"You see this smile?"

First thing I recognized,

the one I've been with.

"You see this?"
Opening the cavity
to his heart.

Bright green glow
signed by Kim.

Tears releasing
uncontrollably.

Sunflower

Never Loved Before

The way
you look at my chaos

and decided
to love me past it

is beyond
my own comprehension.

I don't
understand.

My heart
burns for you

like a candle
with a never-ending flame.

All I can say is
passion.

One day I will.

The Bird's Song

Tweet tweet
toot

the bird sang

That's
a beautiful song,

I wonder
what it means.

The wind gusted
ever so slightly

as I heard
"I love you."

Sunflower

I Fly.

I looked up
toward the clear
blue sky.

A bird soaring
so high

I smiled
and knew.

It had been so long
since feeling

the wind
beneath my wings…

Never again.

Statistical Mathematics

What are the odds

they would
both fall

and open

to the same page?

Sunflower

Tough Questions

Why are you
getting worked up

over an
uncontrollable

that isn't even
in your immediate
life right now?

I've always been keen
to ask myself
the tough questions.

That's how we learn,
right?

I'm not sure,
I replied.

As the clearing energy
in my response took over

at first
I tried to make an excuse,
it messed up my flow.

Was it aligned to do then?

No.

Is it aligned to do right now?

No.

Then why worry?
There was no point.

I felt my frustration rise
then leave
through the top of my head.

The spot that
typically steams
when I get angry
now is open

for this gentle,
clear, loving energy
to be released through.

My crown is growing

time to embody
the Queen.

Remember

keep your composure,
the road you're traveling
requires poise and grace.

Sunflower

A Little Support

Sometimes while we are on our solo path,
we get lonely.

After all we are always doing this solo.

We come into this life by ourselves and
leave by ourselves too.

Yes, we have support of our mothers, like
the Earth Mother who nurtures all her
seedlings

but ultimately, we each have one life to live.

No one else can be along for every moment
of it.

However,

Sunflower

This doesn't stop us humans as social being from trying to reach out and communicate with another this way.

Just don't be surprised if they don't give you the answer you seek. After all, they have different thoughts, emotions and experiences backing up their reasoning.

Support is always going to be there when you need it, just not always in another person.

This support could simply be from Earth Mother showing you the skies have cleared. Or perhaps the wind kissing your face to remind you that you are not alone, you are loved and that everything will pick up again before you know it.

Keep faith.

Opinionated

The voice of reason
doesn't visit me anymore.

That is what
my siblings are for.

Sunflower

Salutations

I walked outside
and was blinded.

"Good morning,
   Kimberly."

"Good morning,
   Sunshine."

Those words
never seemed so natural.

Wish You Were Here

I hug my phone at night,

just to feel closer to you.

Sunflower

Let go and Trust

"I need help!"
I proclaim

"Letting go
and trusting."

"You already have."
I need to see,

I drop an
armful

black speckles
ball to the ground

rising up
as flowers.

Pink petals
yellow inside

they've turned
into beauty

"I need to
fill in."

"My dear
you are

whole and
complete already."

I see
the shinies

Where once
darkness dwelled.

I believe
I trust

Yes yes,
I am.

Sunflower

Impress You

I'm not perfect.

I hold myself to
impossible standards.

I get awkward
nervous and smile.

I want you to like me
& think I'm cool.

But you know me

maybe better
than I know myself.

Suddenly I forgot

how to be me
wild & free.

Insecurities

Yes, we're perfect.

We both have things
we're working on.

I am a recovering
perfectionist

We, my love are
working on us.

I'm very strong minded.

I believe in myself but
sometimes I doubt.

It's not you,
it's me.

It's not us,
it's me.

It's not my past,
it's me.

Sunflower

I failed many times.

But I've gotten back up.
I always will too.

I hold myself
In such high regards
I can't see the top

Then get mad
I can't reach it.

I'm harsh,
I'm hard

But doubt this
Not at all.

I doubt myself

My ability to be perfect

It's all I ever
strive for

It's my weakness.

Then you look at me

With those beautiful eyes
and say I already am.

I get confused.

I don't understand.

Then why am I
So disappointed?

I just want to see
Whatever you see.

Because in your eyes
I'm already perfect.

Sunflower

Sunshine

I turned to God, asked
"Are you God?"

"I am like God."
He responded.

I turned to Source
Not either.

I turned to myself
and saw the Sun

reminded of
the light within.

The fire of light
burning bright.

It made me smile.

You flashed your smile

I found Sunshine
A never-ending supply.

All sunflowers need.

Trust fall

Eyes closed
grass below.

Gentle wind
fills nose.

Flower scents
lavender love.

Trust falls
your arms.

Love,
love.

I embrace,
I finally do.

There's more,
me and you.

I believe
you do too.

Sunflower

Even across
Oceans blue

Nothing will
Stop us now

Love found

Catch me

No don't

Take my hand

Let's jump
Off mountains

Caves canyons

Depths unknown

You're here
I won't fear

Always smiling
At you my dear.

Forever & always

The Warmth
of Sunshine

Sunflower

Surrendering your fears to the universe
and allowing the winds to carry away all
those things that do not serve you.

This allows your soul to open up
to have more light, love, and vibrancy.

With release comes expansion.
Now you have room to grow.

You allow yourself to feel the warmth
of the Sunshine.

You allow yourself to finally be happy
again.

This is it!

This is what I've been working toward.
This is the life I've always dreamed of.

No, it's not perfect, but it is just what I
asked for and that in itself is enough to
allow my path to move forward.

The Sun has healing energy.

It does more than just warm the Earth.

It heals your Soul and fills it with the
aspects you desire.

Logical Knowledge

I don't understand
how you work.

I want to know…

You are so different
than me, yet,

together we just flow.

Sunflower

Presence of Love

I want to love you
until the end of time.

I patted his chest,
smiled and said,

"We'll start right here,
right now."

My King

I fought your goodness,
I didn't understand.

Now I know what
I was missing

was a man.

You were never
trying to change me.

You wanted me
wild and free.

You allowed blooming.

Me to be
me.

Sunflower

Unfolding Beautifully

I am a lotus

Constantly unfolding

the truth of
my own world.

Sunset

I was blinded,
I couldn't see.

Still I walked
into the Sun,

Found warmth
peace, happiness.

Never-ending smiles
belly hurting laughs.

Today is my day.

Today I shine.
Steadily I rise.

Sunflower

My Happy

I gave you control
of my happiness

even though I knew it
didn't belong with you.

I wanted to let you
make me happy.

So when apart,
I allowed myself misery.

I was the happiest
I had ever been
when together.

When apart I just craved
that feeling again.

I still do.

But I understand again,
this wasn't meant
to be yours.

It is a gift,

yes,

but it's my gift to share.

You make me smile,
you make me laugh;

true.

But happiness is nothing
if I can't be without you.

Sunflower

Timing Calls

This is the time for me
to step up and rise

to be the Queen
I know myself to be.

I am strong.
I am powerful.
I am courageous.

But I am also
poised polite and
intelligent

Watch me grow brighter
with every passing day,
calmer by night,

into the hero
the world needs me to be.

I am here for you.
& always will be.

Full Moon

Grandmother
shines full

to tell me

I am whole
and complete,

just the way
I am.

Sunflower

The Scare

I thought I had lost you!

Yes, I'm a bit dramatic,

but you know that's
exactly why you love me.

Now the Sun rises
birds chirp with laughter

singing their songs of a
good day to come.

I glance up
and there we are:

two shadowed birds

flying across
the clouded sky.

Forever and always.

Blooming

Sunflower

I thought part of growing up was being independent and knowing I can do anything on my own. But now that I have started showing my true colors, I understand it is more than that.

Sometimes growing up means reaching out to others when you're feeling down.

The ability to rely on someone else to help calm you when there are storms brewing.

Someone that sees the beauty inside of you and instead of trying to pluck you from where you grew. Or trying to cover you up keeping your beauty for themselves. No, they start shouting from the top of the world,

"Hey, look what I found! This beautiful flower right here, everyone come look at the most divine beauty I've ever laid eyes on in my life."

That someone would say…

"Isn't this flower I stumbled across the most magical and beautiful being in existence to grace the world with its presence?"

It's funny, how I never thought of myself as these things until you came along. Then I thought them of you and you only.

Eventually, you said these things to me so often I started to believe perhaps you were right.

Perhaps, I am in fact not this cold hard mess I was from the start of this journey.

Whenever the skies get dark on my days, you can look to me and I'll look to you just as Sunflowers do.

We'll keep each other bright, lift the spirits of each other. After all, this is everything I asked for…someone to call mine.

I'll put him on a pedestal, as he does me.

Find the Sunbeam even when you run out of hope.

I'll keep you grounded as we can both find support in my roots and strong stem.
We are together now, dear King.

I'll rest your leaves on mine until the very end.

Sunflower

Emerging Heart

My body shakes.
My heart aches.
Magnetic green light

beaming from my chest.
It's growing stronger
getting deeper.

I didn't think this possible
brighter, bigger, fearless
you are divine.

We are divine together,
no needs or wants,
there's more to come.

I lay at peace
knowing you're mine
and always will be.

Connected Hearts

I put my hand
on my chest

and can feel
your heartbeat.

Sunflower

Signs Point to You

Everyone is saying
that it's true.

All my guides
are telling me
it's you.

Love,

you're the one.

My one.

Sweet Tooth

I've never had a sweet tooth.
Not so much into sweets
but your caramel skin
makes me want to eat.

Salted, drizzled or topped with nuts
that smile, oh God.
It's the cherry on top.

The way you look at me
makes me melt
like ice-cream on
a scorching hot day.

Still my favorite flavor
don't care if it's runny,
I'll eat it anyway.

You're worth all the cavities
all the sticky fingers
messy hands too.

My world is sweeter.
I love sweets now
'cause you're my muse.

Sunflower

Butterflies and Bees

Springtime has filled life,
this life with messages.

Bee happy, the bumble assured.
You're free, said the butterfly.

Take the time
to indulge in your blooms,
another bumble sang.

I love this time of year.

Untouched Love

Without ever once
touching your skin
you make me wetter
than I've ever been.

Love bites
my neck.
Shortness
of breath.

Up up higher
higher and higher.
Energy vibrating
every single fiber.

Like a surge
of electricity
keep it cuming
dripping wet

Sunflower

Should be scared,
Wolves bite back
Earth shaking howl
creating our own pack.

No no please
don't stop there.
Together forever
naked and bare.

Sweaty, steamy
sticky and slow.
Wolves mate for life
yeah, we both know.

No matter happens
you're my best friend.
You're my alpha
ride or die 'til the end.

Don't Leave Me

Suddenly
my worst fear

is life
without you.

Sunflower

One in the Same

Yin and Yang
Two completes
creating a strong
foundation for *growth*

Sun lights the way
Grandmother's first half

everything is
flowing together
creating an ARt
true masterpiece.

There is such an ease
when love is true.

Just a smidgen
longer babe
I'll be there
& never leave

I'd wait 4 years
but I'd never say.

Maybe you'll
read it one day.
I love possibility
so much room.

Know your arms
to be my home.

& your smile
holds the key
to my, well…
weaknesses.

With you
I know I can
do *anything*.

Sunflower

I Rise For Love

I thought I needed you.

But I was wrong all along.

All I needed was me and the courage
to sing my own song.

The love you show, the love I care.

No matter where we go will always be there.

You will always be the deepest Soul
I'll ever want to know.

Please don't be afraid to really go
dig in deeper, face your fears.

After all, they only bring you tears.

There is nothing more to cry about
you helped me uncover *myself.*

I hope I've done as much for you
as you've done for me.

But love isn't what you or I've done.
It's the courage to be free.

It is the audacity to stand up and say,
this is how we should be.

Love is love.

Sunflower

Falling Deeper

Every message you send
is a beautiful line.

Tornado Weather

The wind grew stronger
the clouds moved in thicker
covering my dearest Grandmother.

I wasn't supposed to be out tonight,
but I wanted to shine just for you,
you're my special star.

& you're my shiny rock.
Rain began to pour, that's my cue.

I got in my car,
turned the key
the radio blasted.

"I'll make the moon shine just for you,"
and he did,
he loves playing with the clouds
now he knows they tell me stories.

I love being in love
with my very own superhero.
He can bend the world in his favor
and doesn't even realize.

Sunflower

Touching Gift

I can't see the future
just what it feels like.
It feels like you.

Soulmate Song

Have you ever found
someone whose soul
sings harmoniously
with yours?

There is something
so beautiful
about the innocence
and purity that comes
with a bond like that.

Sunflower

Know Me Well

He's the Sunshine
on my bad day.

The only one
who can make me
smile through tears.

The man I can
look at and smile
then he'll ask me,
"What's wrong?"

I've given him
my entire heart.
I'll love him.

Yes.

Connected

I just want to hug you.
Yes I can feel it
I'd love your warmth.

Laying wrapped in cloth
solo, alone, like always
feeling every hug.

You squeeze me tighter
kissing behind my ear.
One day we'll be together,

until that day comes
my gifts will have to do.
You'll hold me in the realm

only the sighted can see
I want to lay here forever
in your arms 'til I sleep.

ASAP, soon my love,
it'll just me you and me
living the life
created in dreams.

Sunflower

Tension of Twos

The air was cool
but the Sun set
warmly on
her face.

Need I remind you
everybody has
their own
opinions?

Neither mad
nor frustrated
but the matter
between the two

grew thick
but not veiled
this fog too
will lift by day,

But whose?
Let's not fight
I only want to
See you smile

Opening Up

Sunflower

I hope you know I am not opening myself
up for the sake of you.

This is for me.
This is for my growth.

Granted, I know you being there to support
me was something I needed to learn that I
had everything I needed to do this.

However, the act is something I needed to
do solo.

Just as I came into this world by myself, a
seedling of hope.

I must also be true to that path I walk, or
have rooted myself in.

I love you so much.
Yes, that is very true.

But I need to be me, and you need to be you.

We can stand tall together, reaching for the
Sun.

You know I love every time it comes.

But if I were to fall or break away, I need to
know you would be okay to stay.

Stand on your roots with your head held
high. Still unafraid to touch the sky.

Her Masterpiece

She is a poem.
Every word
a deeper meaning.
Read into it.

She is poetry in motion
walking talking
form of art

Every action guided
by the divine light

An angel?
Too good to be true?

No.

Just is what she is.

ARt.

Sunflower

I am Complete

I'm done
completely finished.
You celebrate
dancing, waving

more excited
than me.
Mostly cloudy
streaks of blue

winds of change
I welcome you.
Lightning flash
thunder too.

This is right
I know it's true.
What's to come
I cannot see

the path
invisible
one step
before me.

It's coming
feeling chilled
in my bones.

Rest now,
rest.

I am complete.

Sunflower

The Midnight Sun

The Sun falls
as I tell the Moon
good morning.

It is just how we are.
You'll always be
my sunshine laying
your head to rest
as the moon rises
shining her luminous light
across the dusky sky.

I am yin as the Moon.
Cold, quiet, precise,
intuitive, receptive,
high-pitched in tone,
all associated
with the night.

There is a reason
I've been drawn
to the Moon and
why we've become
so close
just as family does.

And you,
you are yang
as the Sun.

Warm, loving, logical,
action-oriented,
lower pitched,
constantly bringing light
and laughter to the day.

No matter where
exactly the day is,
the Sun will
always shine.

Sunflower

I sit back
being warmed by
the lowering Sun,
facing my first love;
she's almost complete.

We'll love each other
until the Sun stops reflecting
rays off the Moon.

We work together
and are worth
so much more
as a unit.

Blessed be
all the Moons and Suns
who forever shine
their beautiful magic
on this world.

Pollination

Come here babe
I need you on top

I already came
said I wasn't going to stop.

Sunflower

Pink Rose Leaf

Blue and pink.

Rainbows and blessings.

You and me.

The magick of three.

Morning Messages

I love to see what
you're going to say
every single morning
the start of my day.

You're not here
but I wish you were
beautiful morning words
from him to her.

You tell me every day
you're falling deeper in love
every word on screen
like a message from above.

My smile, my laugh,
the way my lips curve as I grin
my eyes they shine
igniting your light within

Sunflower

\

Our spark turned flames
before our very eyes
but to wake up next to you
I can only fantasize.

Every word like
a kiss on my cheek.
Wouldn't it be nice
if it could happen next week?

To feel your warmth
touching your skin
quickly my dear
our love would turn sin.

You may not write
in rhyme like I do
but every line a poem
stories of me and you.

I, Perfection.

I saw the moon
knew I was releasing fear.
I stepped into the sun
allowing my skin to warm.

"Can I be warm always please?"

I asked Sun for a hug,
he wrapped his rays around me
embedding himself into my chest.
"My light," I exclaimed.

"You are the Sun,
I was reminded.
You are a gift unto this world,
please shine."

I felt my chin lift.
My teary eyes met a familiar smile.
"Can't you see now,
you are perfect?"

Sunflower

I wanted to argue,
I wanted to fight,
but I knew he was right.

He saw my anger,
& saw my pain
"You are perfect,"
he kissed my forehead
and repeated again.

Conclusion

In a field
of sunflowers

I am enough
on my own.

The Bloom

This isn't about how hard your life has been,
but it is about realizing the strength you've
gained from every moment. My love, life
goes on and you are now standing taller and
stronger than ever.

Be proud. You did it!

What next?

Need that extra Sunflower positive energy sometimes? That's exactly what Kimberly does. She opened Positively Kimberly LLC, in 2020 and spreads positive energy across the world daily.

You can find Positively Kimberly on Facebook, Instagram, YouTube, and more for positivity whenever you need it.

Facebook:
www.facebook.com/PositivelyKimberly.LLC

Instagram:
www.instagram.com/PositivelyKimberlyLLC

TikTok:
@PositivelyKimberly

YouTube:
www.youtube.com/c/PositivelyKimberlyLLC

To set up a private session for card readings, chakra attuning, and other spiritual guidance please go to:
https://www.positivelykimberly.com

"Your reading results are bang on! To the point. Thanks, a billion."

- Kylie K.

About the Author

Sunflower

Kimberly Rochelle is an author, poet and spiritual development guide. She enjoys spreading positivity to those who need it in various forms.

She is active on social media and uses all her channels as a resource to show others the true path to enlightenment isn't all rainbows and sunshine. however, one can still find the positive in each situation.

Her writing is aimed to shed light on the ways of development and growth so others can see no matter if they feel they are lost or are "not as developed" as others, they are exactly where they need to be.

After all, each person is given a different test to take, you cannot cheat this one.

Check out the Positively Kimberly website to stay up to date on all the latest content, thoughts, inspirations, and more.

www.positivelykimberly.com

More Writings by Kimberly Rochelle

Sometimes when you've sprouted through the surface of your new word the winds of chaos howl. When this happens, know you are on the brink of your new day.

The winds teach you to be strong and stay true to your roots, but before you know it you'll spread your petals opening yourself up to the most magical of lights in existence. The one within yourself.

Keep an eye out for more books on spiritual development, poetry, relationships, and love, coming soon.

My Personal Blog

www.PositivelyKimberly.com

Sunflower

Made in the USA
Columbia, SC
21 November 2023

26909058R00105